Mort Krahling was Kent's Miniver Cheevy, up from Alliance, Ohio, to make a life and to keep the books here in this town of rail and river. After a brief stint at the university, he settled in as a citizen wordsmith as well as a sometime dishwasher, proprietor of second hand stores and morning bartender at the Town Tavern where he often greetedand cajoled a gaggle of young poets. All the while, he wrote his poems—we have nearly four hundred. There is an air of privacy about Mort's poems as if they were casual personal notes that he might offer to a friend, over coffee, across a kitchen table. He had the gift of touching things lightly. He was a walker, a day watchman, wandering all over Kent daily, his picker's eye searching sidewalks for that dime or the first line of a poem. His world and the poetry that grew out of it was rooted in the local. He lived out his life in Kent, picking up the threads of voices, weaving them into stories, writing what is at once a personal and a public history. At odds with much in the world, Mort lived most fully in these poems through which he became one of Kent's enduring voices. These poems are his real home.

~ Maj Ragain, author of *Twist the Axe: A Horseplayer's Story*

Bottom Dog Press

An Act of Courage: Selected Poems 1965 – 1998

Mort Krahling

Complete poems compiled by Bill Krahling
Selected poems chosen and arranged by
Judy Platz and Brooke Horvath
Edited by Brooke Horvath

Working Lives Series
Bottom Dog Press
Huron, Ohio

ISBN 978-1-933964-76-8

Bottom Dog Press/ Bird Dog Publishing
PO Box 425, Huron, OH 44839
http://smithdocs.net

Credits:
Layout & Design: Larry Smith
Cover Design: Susanna Sharp Schwacke
Cover Art: Virginia Schaefer
Interior Art "Letters" and
Photo on Back Cover: Susan L. Pope
Author Photo p. 101: Tanya Ackerman

Acknowledgements

Some of the poems included here first appeared in *Shelly's* magazine 1975, and in Mort Krahling's three chapbooks: *The Swiss Cross Mystery* (Ravenna, OH: Three Hawk Press, 1983), *Caught in the Glow* (Kent, OH: Kentworcs, 1991), and *Cuyahoga / Cape Cod: One Year* (Kent, OH: Shelly's Press, 1996).
"Spring: Kent" was included in *A Gathering of Poets* (Kent, OH: Kent State UP, 1992).

Contents

Part Two: The Poet/Cartographer: The Movement Is Off-Map

Part Three: Looking for the Fields

“Letters” Ink and pencil drawing by Susan L. Pope

Foreword

"Planting is an act of courage," Mort Krahling said in one of his poems. He wrote poetry from 1965 until just before his death in 1998. This selection of his poetry is a testament of courage not only to the writer of the poems, Mort Krahling, but to his brother Bill Krahling, who meticulously and lovingly saved Mort's poems over the years. After Mort's death, Bill wrote and phoned friends of Mort for nearly six years, looking for stray poems that had not turned up before. Bill had compiled 384 of these poems before his own death in 2005.

These poems and this book are "[a planted] act of courage" by both brothers.

—Judy Platz

Six Blocks to the Diner: Remembering Mort Krahling

> How will poems bring honor? My career
> Lost to age and sickness, buffeted, adrift . . .
> —Tu Fu (trans. David Hinton)

Mort Krahling was not particularly interested in publication. When he died more than a decade ago, most of his work existed in notebooks, on scraps of paper, and as gifts tucked into letters to friends. His published work consisted of three chapbooks[1] and individual poems mostly in small local magazines. Shortly after his death, Mort's brother Bill took upon himself the task of compiling Mort's scattered poems (almost 400 of them). Ill himself, Bill turned over this manuscript to Mort's longtime friend Judy Platz, who arranged what struck her as a representative selection—poems that, as Judy explained to me recently, "spoke most clearly about Mort and his position in life as a chronicler of himself and his Ohio surroundings," poems that conjured a "vision of a Midwest Ohio. . . from years past." Bill's hope had been to find a publisher, but he himself died shortly after Judy finished her work. The project languished until I thought to check in with Bill's wife Joyce and learned that the manuscript had survived.

As I edited these poems, I wondered what Mort would have thought of this salvage operation. Would it feel like vindication, or too little too late? What I do know is that he would have been grateful for the affection evident in the efforts of a brother and a good friend, determined to keep alive what they could. As for what this collection might do for his reputation as a writer, Mort would have harbored few illusions—"I am very aware of my outsider position," he wrote in one of his letters to me—and he habitually cast a disenchanted eye on what passed for accomplishment in the hothouse world of respectable poetry.

I recall, for example, Mort reading at the Zephyr in Kent in 1992, shortly after I had returned to Ohio to teach. I didn't know him then, and watched indifferently as he moved slowly toward the microphone, a clutch of abused pages in hand. He looked that night like someone who'd seen some hard travelling, and it seemed possible that almost everything of value that he owned was either squirreled away somewhere on his person or crammed into the backpack that was never out of reach. He began with what he told us was something new, written after attending a university-sponsored poetry reading. It was funny—about a couple academics for whom manual labor went out with the invention of the electric typewriter—although it didn't get funny right away. At first, the poem talked about his own work at the Town Tavern, "scouring the sinks" and "stocking / The drop-down Perlich coolers," his good shoes "worn down from hauling / Cases to the basement." He was, consequently, not impressed by the poets from Pittsburgh who could (and did) tell him about work only because "they had witnessed a lot of it."

So much, then, as far as Mort was concerned, for the sort of poetry that won prizes and got one published by a prestigious university press. I remember that, as I listened to him read, I began to like this guy who, like me, had done the sort of work that didn't often impress anyone and who, also like me, didn't care to listen to people who didn't know what they were talking about. Clearly, Mort knew what he was talking about in this brief satire that might have been first jotted down on the back of a cardboard beer coaster between rinsing out glasses and wiping down a bar of "smooth pine stained oak" (which tells you all you need to know about how much a beer was likely to cost in that place, and perhaps how likely you were to find trouble there). You can tell that the poet was used to this kind of labor, for the language is precise (those "drop-down Perlich coolers") and his attitude neither self-impressed nor dismayed.

But it was more than Mort's attitude that spoke to me. Watching his nicotine-stained fingers fumbling those tattered scraps of paper, I grew certain that I had seen him before somewhere. Maybe it was his ducking outside for a cigarette, but suddenly I remembered that when I was a Kent undergraduate in the early Seventies, there had been a poetry reading—the first I had ever attended—at which one of the poets had sung the praises of tobacco, and I now felt sure Mort Krahling was that guy. When the reading ended, I went up to him to ask if this could be so. It was. That had been a few years after he dropped out of grad school, he told me, and just before he opened Airflow Antiques—where, I've since learned, it was almost impossible to get him to part with any of his merchandise.

Back in the Zephyr, I was face to face again with that obscure, self-effacing tobacco fiend who had been the first poet—

bearded, beat, in dirty Levi's—I had ever heard reading aloud, amid laughter and rambling asides, his actual poems. I had been impressed that day, and too intimidated even to introduce myself, yet who knows what part Mort had played in steadying my then-shaky commitment to becoming a poet.

So gradually we got to know each other, recognized each other when some event or chance brought us together. As his poem had made clear, Mort was working at the Town Tavern with its bar of "smooth pine stained oak" (mornings Monday through Friday, Saturdays 1-8). It wasn't a place I went much, especially before noon, but I started to drop by, less for the beer and drear than to say hello or to thank him for his latest hand-written poem or letter. Or we'd meet in a diner he dug not far from where I was living and joke over coffee about his latest misadventures. Eventually, I invited him to read in Canton. As with any event involving Mort, the invitation involved several letters and phone calls to make sure things would go all right, to "set the program," as he liked to say, and to assure him that what he had planned would be appropriate. It also required picking him up and driving him back home. Whether Mort (a) couldn't afford a car, (b) didn't know how to drive, or (c) was philosophically opposed to car ownership, I never learned. It was one of the less important things about him I might have asked on any number of occasions but never did. The smart money, however, is on (a).

Afterward, Mort thought to send a note about the reading to his alumni newsletter. The notice provoked a letter from a woman he had known as an undergraduate but hadn't seen since. She was now a writer living on Cape Cod, and she sent him a copy of her novel *Catching the Light*. Which is what Mort proceeded to do. One letter led to several, and those several to a romance. It was a terribly gentle thing to watch, like something out of Richard Brautigan's fiction. As some of the poems collected here recount, Mort visited her at Cape Cod, and she came to Kent with the spring. Love blossomed with the daffodils, and Mort didn't give a damn about keeping a bar clean. Then the Town Tavern closed and Mort died.

As William Saroyan says in one of his plays, "Things end. That's what makes them things." The heart, then, is clearly a thing. Mort had one and it stopped. But some "things" don't stop—like the grace and humor with which he met the world despite its disappointments and the bad luck it often handed him like a case of empties. He never planned to spend a good part of his life hauling Rolling Rock down to a bar basement, and he never figured on relentless physical breakdown or an early death. But Mort was all right. As far as I ever knew, Mort met things as they were with a willingness to work with what he had, to find it meaningful and enough, and to trust that something better might well be on the way. Such traits are more than things, and you can see them enacted, embraced, throughout the poems collected here.

What else doesn't end? Memories don't. Mort chuckling with me outside the Zephyr over his poem about the Pittsburgh poets, or holding forth for almost an hour on a drive to Cleveland on the Indians' chances for a pennant (on the trip home, he took as his text the Mount Union football team). A Christmas card with a sappy picture of stockings hung along a mantle and inside his penned greeting: "the celebration of the mismatched sox." Mort upset when he got ill the night he was to read from his new chapbook, finding here further proof that as a poet he would always run out of the money but ending his letter "grumble, grumble, grumble . . . Hey, let's sit around and swap 'isn't it tough being a poet' stories." Mort handing me a copy of his first chapbook, *The Swiss Cross Mystery*, with a note scribbled on the title page apologizing for the fact that it was a reprint: "original (esp. w/ signature) valued in low thousands. Sotheby's keeps calling. . . ." And of course my memory of him reading all those years ago and in the process somehow teaching me the obvious: one can be a poet.

Being a poet is something else that never ended for Mort, any more than his having been a poet has an end. He left almost 400 poems. But of course he did, and they're still here. Of course they are. What sort of person ever thought of calling a poem a thing? Or death the end?

—Brooke Horvath
Kent, November 2013

[1] *The Swiss Cross Mystery* (Ravenna, OH: Three Hawk Press, 1983); *Caught in the Glow* (Kent, OH: Kentworcs, 1991); and *Cuyahoga / Cape Cod: One Year* (Kent, OH: Shelly's Press, 1996).

Part One

Memory Jars: The Ohio

Spell

Some rain after a long dry season,
And the river is up, brown water
Above the exposed roots.
Mid-summer brown leaves,
Dry branches toward the falls.
I would make something of this,
A song to float, ashy ink …
I do not move
From the bridge.

8/23/1991

Ohio Geology

Here no dinosaurs prowl
The underground swamps. There is salt,
Some natural gas & meandering veins
Of good thick coal.

Grandpa's plow blade would turn up
Bird points of sharp Ohio flint.
He'd pocket them for the day, throw them later
Into a cigar box. The box
Did not go to any of his children, or show
Up at the auction.

Deeper than blade could plunge,
Animals stalk north water
That turns colors in the long evening.

c. 1976

Vertically

First the clearing of the land
To find the asphalt
Deeply buried. Sifting the sand
Shakes out the aged buildings.
The beauty of mystery is
That there is nothing unused.

c. 1975

Family

I want to wear a shirt
W/ my name on the back &
Sit in Uncle Karl's kitchen
With the pump in the sink.
He to tell me how much butterfat
The Ayrshires produced,
And me, smiling, drinking Uncle Jake's
Homemade wine, looking like Uncle Elmer,
Taking it all in.
(Uncle Elmer worked once,
Drank a lot, and made memory jars.)

c. 4/1975

Wade Street, a Block Away

Goat Hill because of the Welsh
Who lived nearby and played here—
The Quicks, the Morgans, the Mainwarings
Who built the cranes that haul up
The freight in New York
And Toyko, ran for mayor, coached
Basketball, lit a match and killed a
Friend. The East End A.C. wore green
For luck, or Irish, or something, and
Pinstripes for the Yankees. And satin
Jackets, green and white. Here Daubow
Was hit with a javelin in the 30's and in
The head. Here, years later, slow of field,
No hit. The boulder is still there
And part of the hill, a plaque on it.
The empty concrete pool,
The G. I. housing, the ditch and the peppermint
Are assembled and gone. There's a school there,
Called Morgan. It's clean.

4/19/1975

Handful of Pips

Planting is an act of courage:
To bury fertility, to drown the seed,
To shock the apple
W/ Ohio winter and again
W/ timid spring. The planter
Must understand balance,
Must understand that harmony
Is divided before it is one.

7/17/1991

Caseus Helveticus

He called her Mother, then Grandma & she
Had names for him.
                                                  In a cool room
The cheese ferments, is washed, is allowed
To grow old, to hollow out, the emptiness
The proof of growth.
                                                  In Holmes County the farms
Are smaller than the hills, and the cheese is good.
It is ever so; Grandpa found gas on the farm
& moved to the city, such as it was. His son Harvey
Kept forties Cadillacs in the garage; he never drove.
Swiss cheese is a good melter.

6/2/1975

After the Death of Pearl Odessa Miller Krahling

Once the interurban ran here,
Right by here and
Brought a farm girl
Away from the clay pits and the mills
To lilac gardens
And a little normal school.
She in old photos in shining white
Smiling, smiling.

Then, tickets on the same interurban
Back to the grove where
The gypsies camped.
One room and all of them
Beneath the hickory trees.
One year, only one,
And then all of us taking her
With us into the growing soils
Of the Midwest.

The lilac by the corner of the porch
Blooms and blooms again.

2/20/1982

Athletes Dying

They were ours…
Region, symbols, sharing.
Munson, Canton, and Kent.
In '79 flying into the earth.
Olin and Crewes, Tribe,
Oh, this was going to be
The final next year.
            A boat dock, bass
Fishing in spring training.
            Inside page, Victor Smith,
Sophomore DB, flash at football,
Returns home and dies
Of unknown meningitis.

3/24/1993

’93: 14-0

The very name.
A high point reachable
Through working together.
                    The Mount:
A group, a band, a bonding;
                    The Union:
Intense activity, rapid movement;
                    The Raiders:
This ordinary game
            Made extraordinary.

12/29/1993

Good Friday '93

Their history, the family history,
Is mine; I bear the mark
Hidden beneath the skin,
Cannot see it, cannot be seen.
More than name, or size,
Or way of speaking. More than
The nick for a weak heart,
The pattern of being re-created.
This Good Friday, I gather up
All my darkness, touch fingers
To the top of my skull, probe the wounds.
I am self, and multiple. And you, too.

The spring is not yet,
Though a few early flowers,
And the river high.

4/14/1993

I Have, in Years Past

I have, in years past, been to Garretsville,
Edinburg, Randolph, Rootstown. I have walked
The old streets of Ravenna. The hidden places
In Kent—University Heights, the river,
The poet streets around the old high school.
My brother summers in Maine,
Sometimes stops on his way up, or back.
I send him letters, c/o General Delivery,
Kennebunkport.
It is beyond the county, and alien.

5/28/93

As If I Could Desire

As if I could desire extra years—
Fleeing into this coming century—
As if I could be sent boldness in a box,
Return addressed to the proper agency.
And then, w/ extended time
And the courage to learn
Of my own creations,
Rid myself of conditionals,
Paint my face w/ mercy,
Teach rabbits to howl,
Take my grandfather's name—Gottlieb—
Set table for my many selves:
A red-meat meal,
A pulsing wine.

8/16/91

In Alliance

(Read by Bill Krahling at MK's 12/15/1998 funeral service)

In Alliance, at the east end,
State Street
        Runs under the RR overpass,
        Past the strip mines, grassed over,
        And the clay pit-drain tile & brick-
        Fluted points of whit flint,
        Up the long hill to Mount Union
        College and one-time village,
        By the school and leafy homes, thru
        The shopping district of the last century,
        Thru the land-eating new one
Bends off to Canton,
                        Texas at one end,
They said, and Maine at the other.
Route 62, was your spine marked "Alliance Clay"
On the underside?

5/24/97

Spring: Kent

1

It comes, as ever, far after
The time we had chosen.
And even come, some slight chill
Remains. To be found unexpected
Like a box full of old mail.

2

Voices hang in the trees
Along the river, under the bridge,
And I must listen,
Carve out meaning, throw bread
To small white ducks, suck at
Rotting teeth, come home
With a twelve pack of beer, a can
Of Campbell's potato soup. The white cat
Comes out from the trailer hitch.
I feed, he feeds. There is no mail.
In thirteen days
I will be thirty-one. And it's on.
The whole thing is on.
The end-of-the-year suicides hang
In cascades of light. And it's on.
On with the water, the voices in the water,
On with the sunlight shining
Beneath the water. I imagine coils
Of thick wet hair, anchored
Against the current.

5/5/1990

Those Who Own Kent

Those who own Kent, and live here,
Don't live here. Two miles north
in Twin Lakes, and one mile further,
Sugar Bush Knolls—flanking
The ordinary highway, easy access, they say,
To the interstate, to the turnpike, to get further away.

Gray Gables hides from Monument Beach.
A wisp at the end of a private road,
Cotuit more open—they have things to see—
But fading off to restricted beaches.

The old farms around Alliance slipping away.
The remaining barn-red now colors new houses.
Narrow roads widen. Polished trucks go into town
For fresh corn shipped in to the markets.

5/16/1998

Kent

The last grocery store downtown
Became our second city hall—
The houses behind the store
Moved across the street
To the last open land, once farmed.
No longer bagels or bananas
Or loaves of bread, but ripe offices
For part-time council members,
And plenty of parking out back.
Two city halls a block apart,
And 50,000 people driving
To the food fortresses
On the highways to Akron
And Canton and Youngstown.

3/6/1998

Prior to the Modern World

Prior to the modern world,
Kent was smaller and self-contained.
Jobs were here, and homes. Ways to get out,
And several in-trains an hour, the interurban.
Hotels for travelers, the Opera House, dancing
Behind the rose window. Now
We only sleep here, and drive—one at a time—
To where the work is. And where the work is,
There is no living. We knew our neighbors once,
Once lived in a neighborhood w/ sidewalks,
Bought bread and milk from a man
Who lived five blocks from his store.
The store, the bread, the milk gone. The Chamber
Of Commerce bringing in a snail shop.

9/25/1998

Behind Me, Water Heats for Coffee

Over the Crain St. bridge,
A light shines above
The *PD/BJ* vending machines.
On the bridge, the
Dolly Madison/Krispy Kreme trucks.
This bridge is 25 years old.

Over there, to the left,
Lived the first arrivals
From New England.
The new bridge, downriver,
Bears their name,
As does a bar.

4/8/1992

Easter 1992, Kent, Ohio

(for Martin Lovell)

They have been sought by spotlights
From the Main St. bridge. They do not exist.
They do not exist, we are told in the *Courier,*
By responsible citizens. They—not being—are not hungry.
They—not here, not hungry—come to the popcorn machine
Inside the door of the Town Tavern
And eat of the communal grain.

4/15/1992

Multi-Directional

Often the two-way Cuyahoga
Curls through these lines,
North Water Street and the bar
On Franklin, once Canal Street.
Old water, old places,
Carrying to, carrying away.

5/22/1992

And Cold Plums for Dessert

The wine was chosen by
The glow—a directed light.
(If I traveled, I would have traveled
To Amish country for the cheese.)
The pudding bread is mine, round
Above the seasoned pan. I prepare
And am given this meal
Along the river. The flow is measure
Of the gift.

6/12/1991

The Cuyahoga, the C&O in Kent

Two movements below the bridge,
The old Chesapeake & Ohio tracks—
Just past the other bridge they run
15 feet below the station—
The older river, here flowing away
From the lake, running also to the station.
There, beneath the old bridge,
                                        a waterfall.

7/22/1992

Riverwalk

The stone where, perhaps, the running scout
Jumped 20 feet across the Cuyahoga. Maybe,
It was narrower then.
                                        Civil War bridge, now
Spray painted.
                                19th century commerce, shadows
On the water.
                                Here, a new wash of stones
Down the embankment to the river.

7/24/1992

Alliance

The Sourbeck House, by the railroad station
Where Lincoln spoke in the midst of war,
Was torn down 90 years later, 50 years ago.
Nixon came in the sixties—there are
No markers, nothing to remove.

The last downtown hotels closed;
The '50's railroad station, low, thin brick, waits
Down Main Street from the bronze soldiers.
Growing up, I learned time
From the shop whistles—the shops
That built railroad wheels and cranes,
Turbines and door-lifters.

The shops have closed; the tracks
No longer divide. Time is bronzed
In the Ohio skies, now bell blue.

3/25/1998

The Towns—Named for Themselves

The towns—
Named for themselves,
Their homes back east.
Once in a while,
For the peoples they displaced,
Whimsy & history & headlines, too.
Monument Beach for the filled-in
Manomet River, the river
And Manomet people gone.
Alliance—the combining
of 3 villages: Freedom, Liberty,
Williamsport. Later joined by
Mount Union, the college town
On the hill. Kent originally
Franklin Mills, for a settler's son.
The Kents brought the railroad,
The railroad brought the name.

8/20/1998

Once the Roads Came into Town

Once the roads came into town
And carried the names of farm villages.
The railroads and interurbans ran through,
Stations and shops settled in.

At Main & Water, near the banks, the river,
The Opera House—a circular horse trough.
Riders talked & swapped & looked
At the Saturday night skies above the water.

The measure of Time about to change &
The traffic arrows point outward.
No whittling, no walking, only
Artificial light on the water.

4/10/1998

Only Lake Erie

Only Lake Erie, of Ohio waters,
At the top of the State,
Has no other visible side.

I have crossed the Cuyahoga on dry foot
When Akron diverts water to be sold
To the silver ring circling the city.

The Steel River, the Mahoning, in Alliance,
Is a ditch, mossy and thin. The name means
"Salt Lick" in language no longer kept.

On the Cape, the arm reaching into the Atlantic.
There is inland salt; the other side of the water
Is a far away world, old w/ silver moss.

I am from Ohio
And far from home.

1998

Part Two

The Poet/Cartographer: The Movement Is Off-Map

I would begin again, and complete.
May, 1993

Seven Haiku Written During the Rain

I

Soft rains falling on
yearning grass, reaching buildings
and the earth is good
(headline: WRONG MAN IS TARGET OF GUNFIRE
But the rain falls on killer and victim.
They shine dewy-wet,
Spring in their souls,
Tears in their eyes.)

II

The twin mud-brown lakes
reach dirty fingers shoreward
lapping the grass
(The tractors dug and tore,
nature polished,
the scars are gone.)

III

Grass moaning with love,
soft green shoots growing with love
under the rain that loves
(Spring is love.
Clifford Brown knew that.
His trumpet spoke of the grass
Bursting through the ground.
His song: "Joy Spring,"
A song of love and laughter
And silver darts of rain.
A child of spring
And of green grasses
Killed by the silent winter night.)

IV

A small sparrow hops
on the shining wet pavement,
his feet making pictures
(Pictures burnt out by
The sun…beauty of an instant.)

V

I have seen the rain
gently caressing the land.
Will it fall again?
(Joan Baez on the phonograph now.
She hopes,
I hope.
It is all we know,
All we have.)

VI

Small children running
barefoot through warm wet puddles
knowing who God is
(His eyes were brown and
He wore a red striped T-shirt.
"That's a stupid question," he said.
"God is springtime."
Too wise he is.
Someday he'll wonder
And lose his wisdom.)

VII

As I sit, I ponder
reality and truth.
As I ponder, I laugh
    (It's spring: love: beauty . . .
    Wonderful wet green-silver spring.
        Let us run
        Into the rain
        And shout our poems to the sky,
        Smiles on our lips,
        Being as little children
        With wide eyes, and innocent wisdom.
            I know that I am real,
            And those that I love are real
            Because it is raining.)

c. 1965

Once

Once
Was
Isn't now.
An anytime yesterday on an anywhere ridge above
        A half-thought, only imagined lake of maybe blue
Walking with an anybody looking into sometime eyes
Sometime
Somewhere, nowhere, but then no *where*

But there
Here
Near
Very close to a sharp-edged blood letting real
Almost touching almost feeling its planed smoothness
No
Never
An almost, close-by, near to, on the verge of
Nothing
Not
But it was once
Once

c. 1966

The Man Who Looked Like Mark Twain

The man who looked like Mark Twain
Spoke slow   spoke easy.

The man who looked like Mark Twain
Drank more beer than anybody
Except maybe Hansoon, the great Paul Von,
And me at my best.

The man who looked like Mark Twain
Had been or wanted to be
Or should have been
A deputy somewhere south of Dayton.

"Mort,"
Said the man who looked like Mark Twain,
"Look, I'll be seein' you."

It's been 3 years now.

c. 3/1975

Such Things

Such things as I could easily give
Come, perhaps, the hardest, and I end
Simply, as some might say going
For the quick one; a con man.

This too casually done, artless, like
Old songs, or barroom tales.

c. 3/5/1975

I Go to Hear the Poets from Pitt

Bartenders used to wear aprons.
I was damp from scouring the sinks,
Washing the trays of glasses. We still wear
Good shoes, worn down from hauling
Cases to the basement, stocking
The drop-down Perlich coolers. Clean
The back bar in thirds, bottles,
Shelves, mirror, smooth pine stained oak.
Coffee, dark Strohs, vodka & ginger.

The Pitt Press poets told me about work.
They had witnessed a lot of it
In counties an hour drive from the city.
They said they were impressed by it,
And published many work poems.

10/21/1992

Such Men As Are Rarely Noticed

He kept old toothbrushes
In the medicine cabinet
And a bedroom full of beer cans
For future reference.
He counted things
Or assembled them in sets, knowing
How many times the bank clock
Turned in a minute, having
Nearly all the Nero Wolfe novels
In paperback and most of
The Ellery Queens too.
A passion for silver dimes.
He could tell you how many
Different wines from how many
Different countries Kline's Market carried,
And the 1954 Indians' roster.
He hated questions
He couldn't answer and the answers.
He moves among us now, picking up,
Counting. He is not alone.

3/22/1975

Some Stone Circle

Some stone circle,
A hobo's mark / enough!
Of these omens, simple signs / rather something
Concrete
Like that, flat, well defined
Moving about in an orderly way / unmoving
A sidewalk
Not the here or there / the going.

4/9/1975

Today in the Swamp

Today in the swamp by the A&P I saw
Some unknown bird, tan & white, with bent wings
Gliding over where, last summer,
I saw the muskrats diving. Commerce went on,
As usual. The bread scraps in the side yard
Were gone. The furnace was out. Even now,
After midnite, there is a rustle of northern wings.

4/28/1975

The Rye That Failed

The rye that failed to rise—
That I baked flat to feed the birds—
Has reappeared, weeks later,
From the melting snow.
Gray soggy chunks the birds turned down,
Preferring the garbage cans
Or chance. I like that, I think—
The bread, dead from the start,
Dying again, mulching
Beneath the tree, near the oil tank.

2/18/1975

This White Limned Ground

This white limned ground, this design
Pointing toward some coming economic equinox—
A contractor's sand painting of
The bank he will build, here
The west wall (the sign says so), there
The remaining compass, all signed.
Sheaves of iron backbones
Litter the coming driveway.

4/7/1975

The Only Days Have Already Begun

It is a fearful thing, to prophesy
And feel nothing in the hand,
To foretell w/o perception.

The girders of paradise
May be lifted out of
Our visionary discontent.

The hour after the next hour
Is already platted, but we are
Carters of words and not cartographers.

5/27/1992

Going Farther West Than I've Ever Been

There is fear in all beginnings.
Beyond the county line,
There be tygers, beyond
Those in my baggage.
I invent others as companions.
I will not be lonely
On this journey,
Yet I will master
My beasts and run them
Through blazing circles.

4/3/1991

In Time We Stopped Singing

In time we stopped singing,
Turned faces to the ashy door,
And waited.

In time we stopped wearing hats
And went through the door
To the edgy yard outside.

In time the moon rose, and
Caught us in the glow,
Songless, hatless …

Arms uplifted,
We rubbed time in the air
And joyed at the sparks.

1/1991

Birthday Poem

(for Rita)

Startle the day
W/ invented ritual,
Shake loose the sun.
Robe yourself
In morning dreams,
Open the box of imagination.
                                        The air
Is brushed w/ cream.

2/14/1992

Trust

New skin cannot be stretched
Over old, there must be a discarding
… new beginnings lit by tired fires.
Aged wood burns slowly, but brightly
… not the end, but arcing direction.
Fire is a test and a comfort.

7/26/1991

A Moving in Fire

Only this much land, and no more,
No more, as if the land would stretch

Beyond oceans, no more, as long
As the stars shall shine
Or dams hold water, or water falls
The long winter, the longest winter
Settles in, and, hut bound,
Making new curves out of
Old flat things, charts are made,
Vessels built, jewels sold or bartered
Or promised. A moving in fire.

5/21/1975

The Hermit's Handbook

The Hermit's Handbook, page 4, says,
Travel once, travel lightly—
A single bag, waterproof canvas,
Too small for non-tangibles.
You will carry enough sorrow
In those things allowed.
The movement is off-map.

2/19/1992

#9

There are three flowers in this garden,
And I name them.
I can do that. I am
God here.
I laze among them, newly named,
Fingering their abundant aroma.

I take no pleasure in this; I am
Impatient. The names fall w/ the petals,
And scatter at my feet. They will mulch
And grow   and change—
Rose/Iris/Violet—and die.
Perfection moves this way.

And so begin again, begin in melancholy
W/ a taste of the earth on my fingers.

And so begin again. There is an art to this.
I study the simplicity of liberation, observe
The gracefulness of subtlety, make wishes
On the broken petals.

c. 1/30/1991

#8

I have been watched by fish
In their scaled silence
As I wavered between idleness and beauty.
I should gather them up
And shuffle them,
Read their iridescent omens,
Discover, perhaps, a turn of luck
In a turn of fin, infidelity
Bubbling from a gill … see
Shining generosity
In a three-foot stream.

2/13/1991

December 10, 1993 – 12:45 P.M.

After six months, our first kiss.
At the bus stop behind
The Apple Supermarket,
University Plaza, Kent.
                                                            Lovers before
We embraced, touched skin.
                                                            Lovers before
Being escorted down Water Street.
                                                            Writers both,
We took no notes. Closed together
The pages of our new book.
Soft covers,
Unmarked sheets,
Pen and inkwell.

12/24/1993

In My Young Ohio

In my young Ohio, I thought the buckeye trees
Stopped in Youngstown, near the Pa. border.
A cutting taken over the line would wither.
In older Ohio,
I cross the state line in a prop plane
And do not wither.
Transfer at Pittsburgh, small jet
To Providence, bus to Bourne on the Cape. The canal,
Mo Beach, the double century home on County Road, Susan.

Late August morning, Susan has a birthday lunch in Falmouth,
A colleague at the library. I walk to the beach, the vineyard
A line on the horizon. Return up Shore Road—
Spiky pods on the sidewalk, an old buckeye there,
Out of place, yet leafing still.

11/19/97

Progression

A December weekend.
10 days, 9 nights in April.
At end of May, Susan comes
W/ manuscripts, w/ a white
Emily Dickinson skirt & silk blouse,
Comes to stay 6 weeks.

5/13/1994

We Consider Where to Live

She offers an ocean.
I counter w/ a shallow dirty river.
She lives amid (and I have seen)
New homes a century old,
Salt marshes, cranberry bogs,
Clean streets, a gathering together
Of makers and shapers.

Here, the rubber plants have closed—
The air is better, the jobs have gone south.
Two amusement parks call in
Weekend visitors. Seasonal,
Like the corn. Like the corn,
What we make is everywhere, ordinary.

6/29/1994

For the 25th Observance: May 4, 1995

We were without faces
In an unknown place,
Confused with Kansas and Kentucky.
We came after, were come after.
Now long after, some still remain,
Still return. Still. Markers.
On our faces, on the soft Ohio hill.
It only turned warm on Friday. Today
We bring late spring. Those who fled
On Monday—out Main and Mantua—
Return. I look for the young poet
Who read James Wright. In May. Here, in Kent.

3/22/1995

Why We Remember the Blind Greek

The weaver stole the clam-shell
Purple dye, reserved for royalty, dyed
Patiently the thread … more patiently
Worked the thread into the back
Of the coarse cloak. Homer wore it
As he walked the marketplace singing
Of sky-pointing towers and sky-filling beauty.
Letters from shoulder blades to waist:
"Poet One, Athens, Greece."

1/15/1993

All Well & Good

I have no pin on my cap
—"Poet" w/ photo. No card
—Signatures, date, another photo—
Permitting what I have done
For five decades. Questioned
By the poetry patrol, I have not
The documentation. What I have
Given is not enough. "Papers,"
They say, "Where are your papers?"

2/26/1992

Poem for My Brother Ed

Death does not stay (still).
The final song
Nor congested lungs delay.
The Miami and Mad Rivers run quietly;
The carillon gives voice to clearer tone.
Save for the song, there is silence
In the night air over Dayton.

10/7/1998

#161

It all ends at the skin.
The soft outline it forms,
An occupation in time and place.

c. 3/1993

Having Emptied Myself

Having emptied myself, I am discontent.
Rid of fluids and all the odd
Pieces of lumber, I expected
Enlightenment, a step up to Godhood.
This is desire. I am not empty.

2/22/1992

Letter to Alex

Late Night News

Dear Alex –

Coming home late from the store after a long day. Up too late to help/watch Peter at the bakery, and too early to do much of anything except to extend the coffee at the Diner and talk to Kerry about the festival.

But it's payday and so I've got your *Year Book* in a paper bag along with an extra pack of Kool's and some new bread recipes in an old *Gourmet* magazine that I found at Shelly's. (cold—17 degrees—but no wind).

Leaving Rodney's (it's Rodney of course, but easier to add the 's) on Thursday and seeing the book in the window and having Tom hold it for a day.

Last poetry books bought: *Shelly's* (for Ralph and Mike) and *Collected Poems of Frank O'Hara.*

Last Gildzen read: the thing in '70 *Rolling Stone*, but pissed at *Stone* approach to Kent.

Last Gildzen bought: *Into the Sea*, at Dubois, when I still had an office at Sattefield, a suit, and a small folder of published poems. And so, settling in at the desk w/ the book, the Kool's, and a half-case of Milwaukee's Best @ $1.39 a six pack. Then after the first quick reading putting on the *Misty Miss Christy* doing Monk's "'Round Midnight."

The last (and first) time I ever remember meeting Alex Gildzen: sometime—spring probably—in '60 in the parking lot at Music & Speech after a poetry reading. Standing there w/ John Hand, looking for something witty, finally, I think, asking you to autograph *Into the Sea.*

Then of course—after leaving the University and scuffling—losing the book.

Or have I ever sat surly, sour and bushy behind the counter at the Community Store and sold you Janis?

Caught in various musics, I check back to see Feb. 7/9 entries and figure it's time to close.

Thanks & all,
Mort

2/7/75

Part Three

Looking for the Fields

Notes to a History of Music

As speaking was the first defiance of rule,
So with droning: the removal of origin,
The assumption of responsibility. Not
I am, but *I did it.*
Shortly after followed the invention of evidence.

c. 1975

The Hang-Over Drummers

The hang-over drummers
Still went ricky—ticky—brush—brush—boom
While the front line, alto, trumpet,
Double-timed, and other rhythm
Be—dum—bum—bum—bum—sleedy—bum—bum
And either Bud, everything, or Monk, something
And still the drummer ricky—ticky one-two-three-four
As if the union card and sweat were enough.
                    A new man at the stool,
All high hat and bombs.
                    Double time, double time.
Push, push.   All this easiness.
                    Skay—dop, ah yal kool, blee—dow
Pch—chunk, crisp, crisp, blank, crisp, pch—chunk,
Pch—chunk, pow, pow, pow.
                    Showw—dobby—dubby—ump, showw—
Dobby—dubby—how.
Knowing all of this. It is necessary
To Trane.

4/24/1975

Listening to *Traneing In*

You leave me…
The Union Ave. / the two Daveys
And Bela Bartok haunting, his own bluebird
A familiar we could occasionally ignore
As old friends often do. More specific:
The summer Drummer Davey came in
Not speaking, record cover thrown
On the ironing board, spiking
The side immediately again and again.
Ascension
Bela came in and sat, Davey played
The ironing board. Painter Davey
Played and splashed in oil, and I
Tried to get the drift of Bartok.
He threw open the windows
To all the incredible suns
…breathless.

6/27/1975

Alliance, 1964

Sittin' in Glenn Brown's kitchen
Listening

Glenn plays piano
Glenn plays trumpet

Glenn pours out another wine and
Bird plays and plays and plays

c. 4/1975

For Lunch

1
For lunch:
Two cheese sandwiches
On sourdough corn bread,
One brick, one Swiss
One banana

2
John from Piks calls
W/ new releases, but
I've ordered everything
Again and again

3
Right to left:
Country/Western
Musical, Films, Radio, etc.
Humor & Comedy
Big Bands & Reissued Albums, Classic Jazz
New Releases
Trane
Reeds
Herbie Mann
Brass
Miles Davis
Piano
Les McCann
Miscellaneous
Rhythm & Blues
Guitar

4
Or another way:

Martin Mull	Carmina Burana
Blind Lemon Jefferson	John Abercrombie *Timeless*
Stan Getz *Captain Marvel*	Herbie Hancock *Thrust*
Gato Barbieri *Chapter Three: Viva Emiliano Zapata*	Chick Corea: *Where Have I Known You Before*

Jack DeJohnette *Sorcery* Weather Report *Mysterious Traveler*
Blue Bash! Kenny Burrell Keith Jarrett *Death and the Flower*

5
Or again:
Mull
Blind Lemon *Timeless*
Captain Marvel Thrust
Chapter Three:
Viva Emilio Zapata *Where Have I Known You Before*
Sorcery *Mysterious Traveler*
Blue Bash! Death and the Flower

2/18/1975

Notes to the Album by Bob Kidney

Listen—
One night summer 1970 when
I thought all fright shot out of me. This man
Put me next to the desperate fears
That cling and ferment.

6/10/1975

Standing

Next to fading with the only way out up—
There are better dancers, of course, and
Better dressed out near
The end of the edge. Five years
With these changes. Grin fox and lie,
A choir full of tenors, or none, or some—
Bob, hey hey hey.

4/2/1975

A Year, a Thousand Years

A year, a thousand years
No matter / institutions
Create their own
Continuums / standing
Next to fading.
So
Five years for a bar band
Is certainly
Somewhere near equal
To this or that or some other
NEAR THE EDGE
IS THE END.

6/1975

And Gary Somewhere in Michigan

And Gary somewhere in Michigan
Or Georgia with a new hustle,
Rawboned, thin-fleshed, new toothed,
Grinning, skin thin leather—
An outfielder I think—loping,
Chewing slow and wide, the pocket
Frog flashing, the easy step, the peg.

12/16/1974

An Infielder Ponders the Medicine of His Own Arm

Slashed,
It would pump at an incredible rate,
Enough force to light
Cities on specified days
Til the veins collapse,
Eyes closing
Before the dim.

The secret
Is chewing blandness, swallowing entire
Coolness, flatness, passing off fire.

The secret
Is in taste & the bending & altering
& shaping to habit.

It's all in
Not being dizzy at the moment between
Crouch & motion.

1977

Summer Game

(For Bill Polak & Chuck Smith)

"The beauty of the game is in its going on."
—B.P.
"Just that first occurrence / the unrepeated pitch."
—C.S.

It's all we have left.
The whale lies beached,
His bones plucked to make
The outfield wall.

Babe Ruth a beer-truck driver,
Lou Gehrig behind a desk, but kind.
Dizzy daffy and all out of time,
Out of ice and dying and coming out—
It's everopening day.

1977

August: Thursday at the Town Tavern: Baseball Strike

A few from both sides of the desk,
After their last final, come in
To my morning bar to sample
Beers of Canada and Australia. New beers, too,
Ice-brewed to raise the alcohol content.
I serve what I no longer use to make me taller,
Smoother-voiced, able to glide while bar-perched.
I clean the mid back bar to the clack of pool balls,
Listen to Muddy Waters on the juke box. Some window sun.
A postcard to Cape Cod. One pool player
Is bearded and balding and half my half-century.
Neal, the housepainter-writer, waits for the coffee.
"Where is Ted? And what happened to the magazine,
And the poems he asked for? On love and baseball."

8/19/1994

DP

Simplicity is an ease of motion, free
From diagrams, a graceful arc—
Not speech, but single word,
Substantial only in the moment,
Remaining only in reflection.
Sweep of arm from short
To second to first.

3/27/1991

The Baseball Fields in Kent, Ohio

Gene Michael Field in the woods
Behind married student housing, fenced
For the university team. The high school, too,
Has a field on the edge of town,
Hallways empty. At the park,
The oldest fields. A pair, reached
By bridge, circled by the Cuyahoga.
Behind empty DePeyster School,
The basepaths are green,
Soccer goals in the outfield.
Back yards are decked and fenced
For the dog.

10/1998

Looking for Baseball Fields

Goat Hill was at the bottom of the hill
And named for the Welsh
Who built cranes at their countryman's factory.
Right field rose to Morgan Avenue
(Morgan-the-Colonel, lived in the castle).
East End A. C. Jokie's Indians,
Goat Hill Indians.

10/1998

Here in the Midwest

Here in the Midwest,
Formed only, known only
By what is conclusively
East or West and—
In states like Ohio and Illinois—
The South, the people
Don't grow up or mature.
They merely age.
                                        There are sleeves, though,
And cards hid up them,
The farmer tossing his hat
At the home run skimming
The corn row and damn near
Hitting the barn. That farmer
Will walk a whole field of winter,
Feeling the crack in his upper arm, and grinning
Because no one is near.

8/3/75

3 Years, 216 Poems, 50 Years

In a hammock, on Robert Bly's Minnesota farm,
James Wright, listening, watching, came upon
The wasting of his life.
For half my half century,
I have been, and not being. Left the coming years
Behind me, on the diamond at Goat Hill, taped to the bells
At Chapman/Mount Union, noted on the logs at WFAH,
In the empty corner office at Satterfield/Kent.

Now dry, I can only drink water, and want it
To taste of my thin blood.

7/22/1994

Fade Out

There was a fog
And she disappeared
Into it

There was an end
And I disappeared
Into it

There was a fox
Passed slowly,
Slyly across the screen

There was a long fade
To black

There was
An even longer fade.

6/6/1975

(Photo by Tanya Ackerman)

Mort Krahling (1944 – 1998) grew up in Alliance, Ohio, graduating from Alliance High School in 1962. He attended Mount Union College, where he became a member of the social fraternity Alpha Tau Omega, wrote for campus publications, and worked part-time at WFAH Alliance. After completing his degree in 1966, he pursued graduate study at Kent State University. Mort was there during the tragedy of May 1970 at Kent State and was deeply affected by this experience. A well-known local poet who lived the last 32 years of his life in Kent, he is best remembered for his readings at area bars, bookstores, and coffeehouses around town. He also performed with the Cleveland Symphony and was included in the *Gathering of Poets* anthology from KSU.

CPSIA information can be obtained at www.ICGtesting.com
Printed in the USA
LVOW06s0940070114

368157LV00004B/27/P

9 781933 964768